THE ROCK

The Rock

POEMS

Wallace Stevens

COUNTERPOINT

Berkeley, California

COUNTERPOINTS 4

THE ROCK

Copyright © 1923, 1931, 1935, 1937, 1942, 1943,
1944, 1945, 1946, 1947, 1948, 1950, 1951, 1952, 1954
by Wallace Stevens
Copyright renewed 1982 by Holly Stevens

First Counterpoint edition: 2020

Reprinted by arrangement with the Knopf Doubleday
Publishing Group, a division of Penguin Random House
LLC

The Library of Congress Cataloging-in-Publication
Data is available.

ISBN: 978-1-64009-394-2

Series design by Jenny Carrow
Cover design by Sarah Brody
Book design by Jordan Koluch

COUNTERPOINT
2560 Ninth Street, Suite 318
Berkeley, CA 94710
www.counterpointpress.com

Printed in the United States of America
Distributed by Publishers Group West

10 9 8 7 6 5 4 3 2 1

Contents

THE ROCK

An Old Man Asleep

The two worlds are asleep, are sleeping, now.
A dumb sense possesses them in a kind of
   solemnity.

The self and the earth—your thoughts, your
   feelings,
Your beliefs and disbeliefs, your whole
   peculiar plot;

The redness of your reddish chestnut trees,
The river motion, the drowsy motion of the
   river R.

The Irish Cliffs of Moher

Who is my father in this world, in this house,
At the spirit's base?

My father's father, his father's father, his—
Shadows like winds

Go back to a parent before thought, before
  speech,
At the head of the past.

They go to the cliffs of Moher rising out of
  the mist,
Above the real,

Rising out of present time and place, above
The wet, green grass.

This is not landscape, full of the
   somnambulations
Of poetry

And the sea. This is my father or, maybe,
It is as he was,

A likeness, one of the race of fathers: earth
And sea and air.

The Plain Sense of Things

After the leaves have fallen, we return
To a plain sense of things. It is as if
We had come to an end of the imagination,
Inanimate, in an inert savoir.

It is difficult even to choose the adjective
For this blank cold, this sadness without cause.
The great structure has become a minor house.
No turban walks across the lessened floors.

The greenhouse never so badly needed paint.
The chimney is fifty years old and slants to
    one side.
A fantastic effort has failed, a repetition
In a repetitiousness of men and flies.

Yet the absence of the imagination had
Itself to be imagined. The great pond,

The plain sense of it, without reflections, leaves,
Mud, water like dirty glass, expressing silence

Of a sort, silence of a rat come out to see,
The great pond and its waste of the lilies, all
    this
Had to be imagined as an inevitable
    knowledge,
Required, as a necessity requires.

One of the Inhabitants of the West

Our divinations,
Mechanisms of angelic thought,
The means of prophecy,

Alert us most
At evening's one star
And its pastoral text,

When the establishments
Of wind and light and cloud
Await an arrival,

A reader of the text,
A reader without a body,
Who reads quietly:

"Horrid figures of Medusa,
These accents explicate
The sparkling fall of night
On Europe, to the last Alp,
And the sheeted Atlantic.

These are not banlieus
Lacking men of stone,
In a well-rosed two-light
Of their own.
I am the archangel of evening and praise

This one star's blaze.
Suppose it was a drop of blood . . .
So much guilt lies buried
Beneath the innocence
Of autumn days."

Lebensweisheitspielerei

Weaker and weaker, the sunlight falls
In the afternoon. The proud and the strong
Have departed.

Those that are left are the unaccomplished,
The finally human,
Natives of a dwindled sphere.

Their indigence is an indigence
That is an indigence of the light,
A stellar pallor that hangs on the threads.

Little by little, the poverty
Of autumnal space becomes
A look, a few words spoken.

Each person completely touches us
With what he is and as he is,
In the stale grandeur of annihilation.

The Hermitage at the Centre

The leaves on the macadam make a noise—
    How soft the grass on which the desired
    Reclines in the temperature of heaven—

Like tales that were told the day before
    yesterday—
    Sleek in a natural nakedness,
    She attends the tintinnabula—

And the wind sways like a great thing
    tottering—
    Of birds called up by more than the sun,
    Birds of more wit, that substitute—

Which suddenly is all dissolved and gone—
    Their intelligible twittering
    For unintelligible thought.

And yet this end and this beginning are one,
  And one last look at the ducks is a look
  At lucent children round her in a ring.

The Green Plant

Silence is a shape that has passed.
Otu-bre's lion-roses have turned to paper
And the shadows of the trees
Are like wrecked umbrellas.

The effete vocabulary of summer
No longer says anything.
The brown at the bottom of red,
The orange far down in yellow,

Are falsifications from a sun
In a mirror, without heat,
In a constant secondariness,
A turning down toward finality—

Except that a green plant glares, as you look
At the legend of the maroon and olive forest,
Glares, outside of the legend, with the
    barbarous green
Of the harsh reality of which it is part.

Madame la Fleurie

Weight him down, O side-stars, with the
  great weightings of the end.
Seal him there. He looked in a glass of the
  earth and thought he lived in it.
Now, he brings all that he saw into the earth,
  to the waiting parent.
His crisp knowledge is devoured by her,
  beneath a dew.

Weight him, weight, weight him with the
  sleepiness of the moon.
It was only a glass because he looked in it. It
  was nothing he could be told.
It was a language he spoke, because he must,
  yet did not know.
It was a page he had found in the handbook
  of heartbreak.

The black fugatos are strumming the
	blacknesses of black . . .
The thick strings stutter the finial gutturals.
He does not lie there remembering the blue-
	jay, say the jay.
His grief is that his mother should feed on
	him, himself and what he saw,
In that distant chamber, a bearded queen,
	wicked in her dead light.

To an Old Philosopher in Rome

On the threshold of heaven, the figures in the
   street
Become the figures of heaven, the majestic
   movement
Of men growing small in the distances of
   space,
Singing, with smaller and still smaller sound,
Unintelligible absolution and an end—

The threshold, Rome, and that more merciful
   Rome
Beyond, the two alike in the make of the mind.
It is as if in a human dignity
Two parallels become one, a perspective, of
   which
Men are part both in the inch and in the mile.

How easily the blown banners change to
    wings . . .
Things dark on the horizons of perception
Become accompaniments of fortune, but
Of the fortune of the spirit, beyond the eye,
Not of its sphere, and yet not far beyond,

The human end in the spirit's greatest reach,
The extreme of the known in the presence of
    the extreme
Of the unknown. The newsboys' muttering
Becomes another murmuring; the smell
Of medicine, a fragrantness not to be
    spoiled . . .

The bed, the books, the chair, the moving nuns,
The candle as it evades the sight, these are
The sources of happiness in the shape of
    Rome,
A shape within the ancient circles of shapes,
And these beneath the shadow of a shape

In a confusion on bed and books, a portent
On the chair, a moving transparence on the
    nuns,
A light on the candle tearing against the wick
To join a hovering excellence, to escape
From fire and be part only of that of which

Fire is the symbol: the celestial possible.
Speak to your pillow as if it was yourself.
Be orator but with an accurate tongue
And without eloquence, O, half-asleep,
Of the pity that is the memorial of this room,

So that we feel, in this illumined large,
The veritable small, so that each of us
Beholds himself in you, and hears his voice
In yours, master and commiserable man,
Intent on your particles of nether-do,

Your dozing in the depths of wakefulness,
In the warmth of your bed, at the edge of
   your chair, alive
Yet living in two worlds, impenitent
As to one, and, as to one, most penitent,
Impatient for the grandeur that you need

In so much misery; and yet finding it
Only in misery, the afflatus of ruin,
Profound poetry of the poor and of the dead,
As in the last drop of the deepest blood,
As it falls from the heart and lies there to be
   seen,

Even as the blood of an empire, it might be,
For a citizen of heaven though still of Rome.
It is poverty's speech that seeks us out the most.
It is older than the oldest speech of Rome.
This is the tragic accent of the scene.

And you—it is you that speak it, without
    speech,
The loftiest syllables among loftiest things,
The one invulnerable man among
Crude captains, the naked majesty, if you like,
Of bird-nest arches and of rain-stained vaults.

The sounds drift in. The buildings are
    remembered.
The life of the city never lets go, nor do you
Ever want it to. It is part of the life in your
    room.
Its domes are the architecture of your bed.
The bells keep on repeating solemn names

In choruses and choirs of choruses,
Unwilling that mercy should be a mystery
Of silence, that any solitude of sense
Should give you more than their peculiar
    chords
And reverberations clinging to whisper still.

It is a kind of total grandeur at the end,
With every visible thing enlarged and yet
No more than a bed, a chair and moving nuns,
The immensest theatre, the pillared porch,
The book and candle in your ambered room,

Total grandeur of a total edifice,
Chosen by an inquisitor of structures
For himself. He stops upon this threshold,
As if the design of all his words takes form
And frame from thinking and is realized.

The Poem That Took the Place of a Mountain

There it was, word for word,
The poem that took the place of a mountain.

He breathed its oxygen,
Even when the book lay turned in the dust of
  his table.

It reminded him how he had needed
A place to go to in his own direction,

How he had recomposed the pines,
Shifted the rocks and picked his way among
  clouds,

For the outlook that would be right,
Where he would be complete in an
  unexplained completion:

The exact rock where his inexactnesses
Would discover, at last, the view toward
  which they had edged,

Where he could lie and, gazing down at the sea,
Recognize his unique and solitary home.

Vacancy in the Park

March ... Someone has walked across the snow,
Someone looking for he knows not what.

It is like a boat that has pulled away
From a shore at night and disappeared.

It is like a guitar left on a table
By a woman, who has forgotten it.

It is like the feeling of a man
Come back to see a certain house.

The four winds blow through the rustic arbor,
Under its mattresses of vines.

Two Illustrations That the World Is What You Make of It

The Constant Disquisition of the Wind

The sky seemed so small that winter day,
A dirty light on a lifeless world,
Contracted like a withered stick.

It was not the shadow of cloud and cold,
But a sense of the distance of the sun—
The shadow of a sense of his own,

A knowledge that the actual day
Was so much less. Only the wind
Seemed large and loud and high and strong.

And as he thought within the thought
Of the wind, not knowing that that thought
Was not his thought, nor anyone's,

The appropriate image of himself,
So formed, became himself and he breathed
The breath of another nature as his own,

But only its momentary breath,
Outside of and beyond the dirty light,
That never could be animal,

A nature still without a shape,
Except his own—perhaps, his own
In a Sunday's violent idleness.

II

The World Is Larger in Summer

He left half a shoulder and half a head
To recognize him in after time.

These marbles lay weathering in the grass
When the summer was over, when the change

Of summer and of the sun, the life
Of summer and of the sun, were gone.

He had said that everything possessed
The power to transform itself, or else,

And what meant more, to be transformed.
He discovered the colors of the moon

In a single spruce, when, suddenly,
The tree stood dazzling in the air

And blue broke on him from the sun,
A bullioned blue, a blue abulge,

Like daylight, with time's bellishings,
And sensuous summer stood full-height.

The master of the spruce, himself,
Became transformed. But his mastery

Left only the fragments found in the grass,
From his project, as finally magnified.

Prologues to What Is Possible

There was an ease of mind that was like
    being alone in a boat at sea,
A boat carried forward by waves resembling
    the bright backs of rowers,
Gripping their oars, as if they were sure of
    the way to their destination,
Bending over and pulling themselves erect on
    the wooden handles,
Wet with water and sparkling in the one-ness
    of their motion.

The boat was built of stones that had lost
    their weight and being no longer heavy
Had left in them only a brilliance, of
    unaccustomed origin,
So that he that stood up in the boat leaning
    and looking before him

Did not pass like someone voyaging out of
    and beyond the familiar.

He belonged to the far-foreign departure of
    his vessel and was part of it,
Part of the speculum of fire on its prow, its
    symbol, whatever it was,
Part of the glass-like sides on which it glided
    over the salt-stained water,

As he traveled alone, like a man lured on by
    a syllable without any meaning,
A syllable of which he felt, with an appointed
    sureness,
That it contained the meaning into which he
    wanted to enter,
A meaning which, as he entered it, would
    shatter the boat and leave the oarsmen quiet
As at a point of central arrival, an instant
    moment, much or little,

Removed from any shore, from any man or
   woman, and needing none.

II

The metaphor stirred his fear. The object
   with which he was compared
Was beyond his recognizing. By this he knew
   that likeness of him extended
Only a little way, and not beyond, unless
   between himself
And things beyond resemblance there was
   this and that intended to be recognized,
The this and that in the enclosures of
   hypotheses
On which men speculated in summer when
   they were half asleep.

What self, for example, did he contain that
   had not yet been loosed,

Snarling in him for discovery as his
    attentions spread,
As if all his hereditary lights were suddenly
    increased
By an access of color, a new and unobserved,
    slight dithering,
The smallest lamp, which added its puissant
    flick, to which he gave
A name and privilege over the ordinary of his
    commonplace—

A flick which added to what was real and its
    vocabulary,
The way some first thing coming into
    Northern trees
Adds to them the whole vocabulary of the
    South,
The way the earliest single light in the
    evening sky, in spring,
Creates a fresh universe out of nothingness
    by adding itself,

The way a look or a touch reveals its
unexpected magnitudes.

Looking Across the Fields
and Watching the Birds Fly

Among the more irritating minor ideas
Of Mr. Homburg during his visits home
To Concord, at the edge of things, was this:

To think away the grass, the trees, the clouds,
Not to transform them into other things,
Is only what the sun does every day,

Until we say to ourselves that there may be
A pensive nature, a mechanical
And slightly detestable *operandum*, free

From man's ghost, larger and yet a little like,
Without his literature and without his gods . . .
No doubt we live beyond ourselves in air,

In an element that does not do for us,
So well, that which we do for ourselves, too big,
A thing not planned for imagery or belief,

Not one of the masculine myths we used to
    make,
A transparency through which the swallow
    weaves,
Without any form or any sense of form,

What we know in what we see, what we feel
    in what
We hear, what we are, beyond mystic
    disputation,
In the tumult of integrations out of the sky,

And what we think, a breathing like the wind,
A moving part of a motion, a discovery
Part of a discovery, a change part of a
    change,

A sharing of color and being part of it.
The afternoon is visibly a source,
Too wide, too irised, to be more than calm,

Too much like thinking to be less than
    thought,
Obscurest parent, obscurest patriarch,
A daily majesty of meditation,

That comes and goes in silences of its own.
We think, then, as the sun shines or does not.
We think as wind skitters on a pond in a field

Or we put mantles on our words because
The same wind, rising and rising, makes a
    sound
Like the last muting of winter as it ends.

A new scholar replacing an older one reflects
A moment on this fantasia. He seeks
For a human that can be accounted for.

The spirit comes from the body of the world,
Or so Mr. Homburg thought: the body of a
    world
Whose blunt laws make an affectation of mind,

The mannerism of nature caught in a glass
And there become a spirit's mannerism,
A glass aswarm with things going as far as
    they can.

Song of Fixed Accord

Rou-cou spoke the dove,
Like the sooth lord of sorrow,
Of sooth love and sorrow,
And a hail-bow, hail-bow,
To this morrow.

She lay upon the roof,
A little wet of wing and woe,
And she rou-ed there,
Softly she piped among the suns
And their ordinary glare,

The sun of five, the sun of six,
Their ordinariness,
And the ordinariness of seven,
Which she accepted,
Like a fixed heaven,

Not subject to change . . .
Day's invisible beginner,
The lord of love and of sooth sorrow,
Lay on the roof
And made much within her.

The World as Meditation

J'ai passé trop de temps à travailler mon violon, à voyager. Mais l'exercice essentiel du ompositeur— la méditation—rien ne l'a jamais suspendu en moi . . . Je vis un rêve permanent, qui ne s'arrête ni nuit ni jour.

GEORGES ENESCO

Is it Ulysses that approaches from the east,
The interminable adventurer? The trees are
    mended.
That winter is washed away. Someone is
    moving

On the horizon and lifting himself up above it.
A form of fire approaches the cretonnes of
    Penelope,
Whose mere savage presence awakens the
    world in which she dwells.

She has composed, so long, a self with which
   to welcome him,
Companion to his self for her, which she
   imagined,
Two in a deep-founded sheltering, friend and
   dear friend.

The trees had been mended, as an essential
   exercise
In an inhuman meditation, larger than her own.
No winds like dogs watched over her at night.

She wanted nothing he could not bring her
   by coming alone.
She wanted no fetchings. His arms would be
   her necklace
And her belt, the final fortune of their desire.

But was it Ulysses? Or was it only the
  warmth of the sun
On her pillow? The thought kept beating in
  her like her heart.
The two kept beating together. It was only day.

It was Ulysses and it was not. Yet they had met,
Friend and dear friend and a planet's
  encouragement.
The barbarous strength within her would
  never fail.

She would talk a little to herself as she
  combed her hair,
Repeating his name with its patient syllables,
Never forgetting him that kept coming
  constantly so near.

Long and Sluggish Lines

It makes so little difference, at so much more
Than seventy, where one looks, one has been
    there before.

Wood-smoke rises through trees, is caught in
    an upper flow
Of air and whirled away. But it has been
    often so.

The trees have a look as if they bore sad names
And kept saying over and over one same,
    same thing,

In a kind of uproar, because an opposite, a
    contradiction,
Has enraged them and made them want to
    talk it down.

What opposite? Could it be that yellow
   patch, the side
Of a house, that makes one think the house
   is laughing;

Or these—escent—issant pre-personae: first fly,
A comic infanta among the tragic drapings,

Babyishness of forsythia, a snatch of belief,
The spook and makings of the nude
   magnolia?

... Wanderer, this is the pre-history of
   February.
The life of the poem in the mind has not yet
   begun.

You were not born yet when the trees were
   crystal
Nor are you now, in this wakefulness inside
   a sleep.

A Quiet Normal Life

His place, as he sat and as he thought, was not
In anything that he constructed, so frail,
So barely lit, so shadowed over and naught,

As, for example, a world in which, like snow,
He became an inhabitant, obedient
To gallant notions on the part of cold.

It was here. This was the setting and the time
Of year. Here in his house and in his room,
In his chair, the most tranquil thought grew
    peaked

And the oldest and the warmest heart was cut
By gallant notions on the part of night—
Both late and alone, above the crickets' chords,

Babbling, each one, the uniqueness of its
    sound.
There was no fury in transcendent forms.
But his actual candle blazed with artifice.

The Course of a Particular

Today the leaves cry, hanging on branches
    swept by wind,
Yet the nothingness of winter becomes a
    little less.
It is still full of icy shades and shapen snow.

The leaves cry . . . One holds off and merely
    hears the cry.
It is a busy cry, concerning someone else.
And though one says that one is part of
    everything,

There is a conflict, there is a resistance
    involved;
And being part is an exertion that declines:
One feels the life of that which gives life as
    it is.

The leaves cry. It is not a cry of divine
    attention,
Nor the smoke-drift of puffed-out heroes,
    nor human cry.
It is the cry of leaves that do not transcend
    themselves,

In the absence of fantasia, without meaning
    more
Than they are in the final finding of the ear,
    in the thing
Itself, until, at last, the cry concerns no one
    at all.

Final Soliloquy of the Interior Paramour

Light the first light of evening, as in a room
In which we rest and, for small reason, think
The world imagined is the ultimate good.

This is, therefore, the intensest rendezvous.
It is in that thought that we collect ourselves,
Out of all the indifferences, into one thing:

Within a single thing, a single shawl
Wrapped tightly round us, since we are poor,
    a warmth,
A light, a power, the miraculous influence.

Here, now, we forget each other and ourselves.
We feel the obscurity of an order, a whole,
A knowledge, that which arranged the
    rendezvous,

Within its vital boundary, in the mind.
We say God and the imagination are one . . .
How high that highest candle lights the dark.

Out of this same light, out of the central mind,
We make a dwelling in the evening air,
In which being there together is enough.

The Rock

Seventy Years Later

It is an illusion that we were ever alive,
Lived in the houses of mothers, arranged
    ourselves
By our own motions in a freedom of air.

Regard the freedom of seventy years ago.
It is no longer air. The houses still stand,
Though they are rigid in rigid emptiness.

Even our shadows, their shadows, no longer
    remain.
The lives these lived in the mind are at an end.
They never were . . . The sounds of the guitar

Were not and are not. Absurd. The words
   spoken
Were not and are not. It is not to be believed.
The meeting at noon at the edge of the field
   seems like

An invention, an embrace between one
   desperate clod
And another in a fantastic consciousness,
In a queer assertion of humanity:

A theorem proposed between the two—
Two figures in a nature of the sun,
In the sun's design of its own happiness,

As if nothingness contained a métier,
A vital assumption, an impermanence
In its permanent cold, an illusion so desired

That the green leaves came and covered the
    high rock,
That the lilacs came and bloomed, like a
    blindness cleaned,
Exclaiming bright sight, as it was satisfied,

In a birth of sight
The blooming and the musk
Were being alive, an incessant being alive,
A particular of being, that gross universe.

II

The Poem as Icon

It is not enough to cover the rock with leaves.
We must be cured of it by a cure of the ground
Or a cure of ourselves, that is equal to a cure

Of the ground, a cure beyond forgetfulness.
And yet the leaves, if they broke into bud,
If they broke into bloom, if they bore fruit,

And if we ate the incipient colorings
Of their fresh culls might be a cure of the
    ground.
The fiction of the leaves is the icon

Of the poem, the figuration of blessedness,
And the icon is the man. The pearled chaplet
    of spring,
The magnum wreath of summer, time's
    autumn snood,

Its copy of the sun, these cover the rock.
These leaves are the poem, the icon and the man.
These are a cure of the ground and of
    ourselves,

In the predicate that there is nothing else.
They bud and bloom and bear their fruit
    without change.
They are more than leaves that cover the
    barren rock.

They bud the whitest eye, the pallidest sprout,
New senses in the engenderings of sense,
The desire to be at the end of distances,

The body quickened and the mind in root.
They bloom as a man loves, as he lives in love.
They bear their fruit so that the year is known,

As if its understanding was brown skin,
The honey in its pulp, the final found,
The plenty of the year and of the world.

In this plenty, the poem makes meanings of
   the rock,
Of such mixed motion and such imagery
That its barrenness becomes a thousand
   things

And so exists no more. This is the cure
Of leaves and of the ground and of ourselves.
His words are both the icon and the man.

III

Forms of the Rock in a Night-Hymn

The rock is the gray particular of man's life,
The stone from which he rises, up—and—ho,
The step to the bleaker depths of his descents . . .

The rock is the stern particular of the air,
The mirror of the planets, one by one,
But through man's eye, their silent rhapsodist,

Turquoise the rock, at odious evening bright
With redness that sticks fast to evil dreams;
The difficult rightness of half-risen day.

The rock is the habitation of the whole,
Its strength and measure, that which is near,
   point A
In a perspective that begins again

At B: the origin of the mango's rind.
It is the rock where tranquil must adduce
Its tranquil self, the main of things, the mind,

The starting point of the human and the end,
That in which space itself is contained, the gate
To the enclosure, day, the things illumined

By day, night and that which night illumines,
Night and its midnight-minting fragrances,
Night's hymn of the rock, as in a vivid sleep.

St. Armorer's Church
from the Outside

St. Armorer's was once an immense success.
It rose loftily and stood massively; and to lie
In its church-yard, in the province of
    St. Armorer's,
Fixed one for good in geranium-colored day.

What is left has the foreign smell of plaster,
The closed-in smell of hay. A sumac grows
On the altar, growing toward the lights,
    inside.
Reverberations leak and lack among holes . . .

Its chapel rises from Terre Ensevelie,
An ember yes among its cindery noes,
His own: a chapel of breath, an appearance
    made
For a sign of meaning in the meaningless,

No radiance of dead blaze, but something seen
In a mystic eye, no sign of life but life,
Itself, the presence of the intelligible
In that which is created as its symbol.

It is like a new account of everything old,
Matisse at Vence and a great deal more than
    that,
A new-colored sun, say, that will soon
    change forms
And spread hallucinations on every leaf.

The chapel rises, his own, his period,
A civilization formed from the outward blank,
A sacred syllable rising from sacked speech,
The first car out of a tunnel en voyage

Into lands of ruddy-ruby fruits, achieved
Not merely desired, for sale, and market things
That press, strong peasants in a peasant world,
Their purports to a final seriousness—

Final for him, the acceptance of such prose,
Time's given perfections made to seem like
  less
Than the need of each generation to be itself,
The need to be actual and as it is.

St. Armorer's has nothing of this present,
This *vif*, this dizzle-dazzle of being new
And of becoming, for which the chapel
  spreads out
Its arches in its vivid element,

In the air of newness of that element,
In an air of freshness, clearness, greenness,
  blueness,
That which is always beginning because it is
  part
Of that which is always beginning, over and
  over.

The chapel underneath St. Armorer's walls,
Stands in a light, its natural light and day,
The origin and keep of its health and his own.
And there he walks and does as he lives and
    likes.

Note on Moonlight

The one moonlight, in the simple-colored night,
Like a plain poet revolving in his mind
The sameness of his various universe,
Shines on the mere objectiveness of things.

It is as if being was to be observed,
As if, among the possible purposes
Of what one sees, the purpose that comes first,
The surface, is the purpose to be seen,

The property of the moon, what it evokes.
It is to disclose the essential presence, say,
Of a mountain, expanded and elevated almost
Into a sense, an object the less; or else

To disclose in the figure waiting on the road
An object the more, an undetermined form
Between the slouchings of a gunman and a
    lover,
A gesture in the dark, a fear one feels

In the great vistas of night air, that takes this
    form,
In the arbors that are as if of Saturn-star.
So, then, this warm, wide, weatherless
    quietude
Is active with a power, an inherent life,

In spite of the mere objectiveness of things,
Like a cloud-cap in the corner of a
    looking-glass,
A change of color in the plain poet's mind,
Night and silence disturbed by an interior
    sound,

The one moonlight, the various universe, intended
So much just to be seen—a purpose, empty
Perhaps, absurd perhaps, but at least a purpose,
Certain and ever more fresh. Ah! Certain, for sure . . .

The Planet on the Table

Ariel was glad he had written his poems.
They were of a remembered time
Or of something seen that he liked.

Other makings of the sun
Were waste and welter
And the ripe shrub writhed.

His self and the sun were one
And his poems, although makings of his self,
Were no less makings of the sun.

It was not important that they survive.
What mattered was that they should bear
Some lineament or character,

Some affluence, if only half-perceived,
In the poverty of their words,
Of the planet of which they were part.

The River of Rivers
in Connecticut

There is a great river this side of Stygia,
Before one comes to the first black cataracts
And trees that lack the intelligence of trees.

In that river, far this side of Stygia,
The mere flowing of the water is a gaiety,
Flashing and flashing in the sun. On its banks,

No shadow walks. The river is fateful,
Like the last one. But there is no ferryman.
He could not bend against its propelling force.

It is not to be seen beneath the appearances
That tell of it. The steeple at Farmington
Stands glistening and Haddam shines and sways.

It is the third commonness with light and air,
A curriculum, a vigor, a local abstraction . . .
Call it, once more, a river, an unnamed flowing,

Space-filled, reflecting the seasons, the
   folk-lore
Of each of the senses; call it, again and again,
The river that flows nowhere, like a sea.

Not Ideas About the Thing
but the Thing Itself

At the earliest ending of winter,
In March, a scrawny cry from outside
Seemed like a sound in his mind.

He knew that he heard it,
A bird's cry, at daylight or before,
In the early March wind.

The sun was rising at six,
No longer a battered panache above snow . . .
It would have been outside.

It was not from the vast ventriloquism
Of sleep's faded papier-mâché . . .
The sun was coming from outside.

That scrawny cry—it was
A chorister whose c preceded the choir.
It was part of the colossal sun,

Surrounded by its choral rings,
Still far away. It was like
A new knowledge of reality.

COUNTERPOINTS